The Oaks

by

Craig Neesam & Friends

THE OAKS

Published by CBS Green Man Publications
In August 2017
On behalf of Invisible Voices of Brighton & Hove
as part of the Invisible Voices 2017 programme
for the BRIGHTON FRINGE FESTIVAL 2017
ISBN: 9789082323894

Author: Craig Neesam & Friends
Editors: Nils Visser, Cair Emma, Janet Going, John Going

This book is dedicated to my daughter Maicie and her sister Poppy.

In loving memory of Elvis Monaghan

Contents

Foreword

Invisible Voices of Brighton & Hove was founded in 2015 to offer a platform for those voices in our community which often remain unheard. As part of Invisible Voice's contribution to the 2016 Brighton Fringe Festival a book was published: *Invisible Voices of Brighton and Hove*. Apart from stories, interviews and reports the book also contained many poems, some kindly donated by nationally renowned poets but many 'street' poems by homeless or ex-homeless wordsmiths. This included poems written in the creative writing sessions sponsored by Cascade Creative Recovery. Of the latter Craig Neesam's poetry stood out, filled with heartfelt raw tenacity reflecting a turbulent life of ups and downs.

Invisible Voices offered to publish Craig's poetry in a debut poetry collection titled *Born and Bred* which instantly became our Fringe 2016 bestseller. To his surprise and delight Craig's words were much appreciated and he received invitations to recite his work on local radio and other gatherings around Brighton. Fortunately he didn't forget his roots and he was happy to contribute more work for our Fringe 2017 book, *Invisible Voices 2017,* as well as performing some of his work for the Fringe stage show organised by Invisible Voices and Cascade Creative Recovery at St Luke's in Prestonville.

Having composed a great many new poems he was also pleased when we offered to once again publish a collection of his work, the sale of which would be used to support local homeless and recovery charities. Generous as ever, he insisted on sharing this platform with others. It is for this reason that *The Oaks* contains new poems from other contributors to *Invisible Voices 2017* such as the talented poets Jovannah Bär and RM Bodley, respectively young and young at heart. Craig also invited fellow poets from the Cascade Creative Recovery writing group to share the spotlight, as well as others whose creative output had touched his heart.

Both Invisible Voices and Cascade Creative Recovery are immensely proud of the end product: *The Oaks*. All of the poetry in this collection has been inspired by a range broad life experiences which reflect lives of love and loathing, hope and despair, as well as personal victories and defeats. As such, it is genuine; it doesn't get much more real than this. Craig Neesam and Friends have not been offered an easy stroll through a rose garden, rather, they have had to hack their own paths through the near impenetrable jungle of modern life and have emerged all the stronger for it.

Reading through the poems, I am much minded of Tupac Shakur's *The Rose that Grew from Concrete*. Like Shakur's miraculous rose which grew where this was deemed impossible, our poets too have learned how to walk without feet and dream their way to something better. To honour them I would like to borrow Shakur's words to end this introduction: "*Long live the rose that grew from concrete, when no one else ever cared.*"

Nils Nisse Visser, Brighton, August 2017

Craig Part One

The Oaks

I've found my place,
ADHD is the diagnosis.
A special case, read my mind
Or is it written across my face
See, you would think it's about healing,
My hurt near death
Prison in my mind
I would flirt,
Changing how I feel
Chasing a life or chasing a skirt
Mind altering substance I'd insert
But The Oaks is where I found my church
Caught in between the street and a fucking war
I peeled my self-worth off a stone cold floor
Ya eyeballs couldn't take what I saw
Good times are here, pain no more
So I sit with a pen and a pad
To try work out where it all went wrong
Or did it all work out right,
Cos here I am with my feelings set alright
I don't know if it's a could or is it my survival
That might set this moon ablaze

And then I'll find my true self through this haze.
And I'll be back with her one day.
The seasons are in change,
Can I find a way to illuminate
My state of play,
And she is yet my prize.
I try to rely on an old front
That carries me in disguise
My sin is in protection
By sweet chords from a violin
Do I need to tell you where I've really been?
My mind travels to infinity,
Riches and joys I've seen 42 years
As I tell you this truth will my memory
Make a golden plaque on a park bench?
Or will it be disregarded,
Thrown away, buried in a trench,
But this I've known, I've held love by my hand,
My fist I've clenched and so my final song
Did I really get it wrong?
Or was it mapped out like this all along.
Either way, please let sweet chords play
So she knows as I say goodbye
And with that last breath maybe: Hello.

25

Welcome to my peace, although I long for release.
She said "don't give up",
I longed for her touch,
I've never been so in love.
There ain't no truth when my pen touches you there
There ain't no ----
A yearning within protecting my kin,
Say "stay" say "with me".
Addiction on my back, draw, pull, attack.
My soul is cracked, hello, goodbye.
Succeed, take it back, I mean
It hurts, I'm tired, I'm alive but I don't cry
My shadow is cold, my inner peace has been sold.
Long day, why didn't I stay?
Pain doesn't go away; I just make room for it.

A Journey of Peace

We may think we are through with the past
But the past will cast
A shadow of disbelief,
Which as an adult will move in fast.
We can't stop it.
The suns not going down on this one
It may not be about the acts that were done
It's about acknowledging
The pain, resistance, loneliness when young
Giving up is not the same as becoming undone.
Victory comes when throwing in the towel
Our essence takes in our mothers tongue
Choose our own words, choose our vowels.
Cos when we are floored and life drifts unmoored
The battle is not external, it's an internal war
But the voices sound the same
And the scars from the warfare remain.
We need to revisit adolescence with a white flag
And a blanket to wrap around the shame
For we don't rename shame, we salute and claim it.
We certainly don't blame it.
We only aim for peace on our journey

That a few will call a game.
So, on this road it doesn't matter
Where you start to discover
One's self must be the art, academics, scholars.
The smartest soul knows
Their heart in this mortal body will one day cease
Don't look to the sky or others outside for release
Take a look inside for you have the answers.
You are the journey of peace.

A Wink

Born, conditioned in our primary,
Some will keep a diary
While others rely on their memory
Either way we regret,
Try to forget the fears and pain
Of yesterday.
Born, fed we are led,
No instruction manual to be read,
A third of our lives spent in our bed.
Some will comprehend,
The magic of making a friend
While the separate will stay angry,
Alone, sad till the end.

The value of finding a special one
Isn't to produce a daughter or a son,
It's the child that produces a father and a mum.
Is it fate? Born too late
Spoken word empowers others to create
Originality is you, no need to duplicate.
So in this life do you add or subtract,
Do you attract or re-enact,

Are you happy with your latest phone,
Tablet contract?
With ya Facebook,
Tinder contacts
Searching for what?
Is that even a matter of fact?

Some will pray and I don't mean on their knees
With hands clenched, everyday
I mean in a way where people are running
Scared and afraid
So as I read you this spoken word,
As you sit
In your own life,
Are you really happy with it?
Or do you wish you were magical and a poet.
Well fucking check this out,
You're more than beautiful
Just look inside and you'll find it
So know, pause, think, smile, love
And don't forget to give each other a wink.

Abandoned Nights

I count days until she is mine
And holding her, there is no time
Her love so lean too, that I serve
For my heart has no name but reserve
Whispers of the night sing softly her name
Dreams disappear without a trace
Like a flame to pull me through each fight
She is my motive
And I would die for this beauty to live
Lonely planets spin around my birth place
Their light shines on me as I cry for her face.

Attraction 1

CO2 and the government blames you,
Tax will rise and it's a disguise
But they give us the lottery.
What they're really doing behind,
We need to open our eyes
As advertisements tell us
We're fulfilling from outside,
Let's not keep quiet, no need to hide.
Smartphones evolving to lessen human contact,
Children separated from playful interact.
Divided souls in isolation a startling fact
Quick fix world,
The lonely heart kept up late at night,
A careless swipe that's Tinder choice,
Quickly swipe left or right.
Prolonging of life, many try to break the code,
Fake news is spread and rumours are told.
Consumerism 24/7, law of attraction, self-powered,
Driven, online dating, a lonely hearts heaven.
Meat grinder crematorium,
The death of a technical citizen,
"Hotel Trivago" but you can't see their prison.

And people wake to an insidious blank expression,
Is it any surprise they use a mood altering substance
To ease the tension.
Log in, search for a common condition,
Therapy sessions,
London underground in a sour disposition.
Clouds of lust hang over us;
Sunday's new church is EastEnders omnibus.
In each of our minds lays a trap,
It is the delusion that our habitat
Is held down with straps.
With thinking that is black,
The human condition is under attack.
Take control don't leave it up to the zodiac,
You behave, you feel, you think, you attract.

Attraction 2

When did I become so cold?
Was I born in shame?
I've waited too long to roll this dice in this game
It was taking over me, voices crying
Am I sane?
No sun shined, I only had dark days
There must be another way
The lonely days were not a fact
It was in my thought that I would attract
For my mind affected,
My fears then backed by my behaviour
All had a massive impact
The origin was my power of attraction
I thought of sadness and pain
It was an internal transaction
I would listen to love songs and repeat this action
I needed to change
This thought pattern and behaviour
For this would be life altering saviour
I could finally see that what I believed
Would manifest to what I would be
I only thought of a lie,

The truth is that I'm a decent guy
There is no indecision of try
And if I didn't follow a manmade religion
I would spiritually die
What I believed would definitely reach me
I wish you could see.

Can you

Can you hear the lonely cry?
Of the lost soul in the midnight sky?
Can you see God's creation lay in a heap?
Do you see their face as you try to sleep?
Can you smell the actions of a sin?
Is your nose in the air? Patience runs thin.
Can you give to someone so lost?
Do you love? Does it come at a cost?
Can you touch a wanting hand?
Lowering yourself so the desperate can stand?
Can you emerge as one with your brother?
Your mother, father, daughter, your son?
Can you show friendship like never before?
Will you welcome a stranger and open your door?
Can you taste the fear in a voice?
Shattered, abandoned, alone without a choice
Can you have an unseen faith?
Will you give an unknown your day?
Can you make contact with the untouchable?
Can you open your mind? Is that possible?

Control

I'm staring at the sky
When you're staring at the floor
I'm seeing an open field
And all you see is a closed door.
You sense less when all I feel is more.
I'm letting off a smile when I look at you
Looks like you're on trial.
When I speak of this world's beauty
You frown then proceed to disagree.
When I'm walking on a fine golden beach
Your soul is broken, you long, you reach.
Things that come to me are so sweet
You walk these streets, you're so angry
You fight, you beat, so judgemental,
You tell the world in a tweet.
I'm connected and my life is one,
You just give up and say 'I'm done'.
My attitude is fun, you fucking got none,
Just a poisonous tongue.
When I ask you why, you just blame everyone.
I work from the inside out;
You look within and question,

Doubt, then proceed to shout.
I'm up and ready, I'm out and about,
When morning comes your daytime telly,
A sofa layabout.
It's like your will to go get a life
Is in big time drought.
See some people will come drop beauty at our feet
Every day on our street.
We are driven to believe we are incomplete
Don't forget your ten a day as you eat.
Is it really a coincidence?
That in the centre of each person
Is grace or do you spot indifference?
Where are you investing,
Have you true providence I wonder.
Why you live with so much control when happiness
And freedom comes when we let go.
There is not a dam or blockage to contentment.
It is in the centre of us all
We must let it in to let it flow.

No Enemy

A day will come when painful hearts
Will open and become undone
For this moment you will never be so young
A day in which icebergs of anguish
Disappear and melt away
And rapture and delight are here to stay.
Finally you will find your path
You will find your way
Regret you will laugh and joyfully play
You will realise the past was not wasted
For you showed courage, pain you faced
The rewards of which today,
Infusions of grandeur you taste
A place where hurt has overcome you.
Tell the truth to the young
And laws of attraction are carried out
For freedom has begun.
Warmth is spread over a forgiving sun
There'll be no tears over pointless years
And courage shines through the lies of fears
There'll be no fantasy of over a rainbow,
For in each soul you will sense

Riches more than gold.

Every story will be told

A being searches for a love

At the earth's top and stops at not

Most of us are searching for we have already got

And we live with regret watching

These consuming issues eat us alive.

Nothing can be bought to fix what's inside.

No enemy inside then the enemy outside

Can do us no harm.

First Friendly Interlude

**Poetry by Sarah Daniels, Janette Bryan
& Paul Delaware**

'Desperate People!' by Sarah Daniels

Fag butts, old sluts,
Desperate people,
Dark places
No eye contact,
Broken faces,
Pain in our hearts
Shoes no laces,
Crack walk races,
Walking alone
No mobile phone
No place to call home.
Short path long road,
Crack whore for a score
Don't want to live no more!
Pipe smoke,
Deep breath,
No hope left.

'LET GO, MOVE ON' by Janette Bryan

Forward thinking, dreaming,
Living as I pass the people who are stuck in time
Crying, weeping shouting
"Help me I can't do this on my own
"Help me please I'm sinking, drowning dying"
In a state of upset created by oneself
"Help me, save me hold me don't let go
You have to save, please don't go"
I'm not leaving but I won't save you
I'll guide and cheer you on
You have the answers you have the tools
Now stop the crying and think what you can do
You're bright and beautiful
Now check out those tools
Don't just carry a closed bag around with you
"I can't I'm scared don't be so unfair
I can't do it without you"
Now stop that and look back
At how far you've come
Did I carry you this far oh hell no
You got hear you did it one step at a time
Look up open your eyes coz you're not blind

Now look up look ahead it's time to face those fears
Check out are they really there?
Anxiety and fear can hold you right here
It's your choice to remain and be scared
One step at a time put that in your mind
Make a choice, you can stay or move on
Look to your side you are not alone
We're all here cheering you on

We can't walk your walk for you
Or chose which tool to use
But I'll walk right along next you
Leave some of the bags and I'll carry a few
Do you really need all of those with you
Everything that you need put in these 2 or 3
It'll be easier to walk wait and see
We all need to leave some of the past in the past
Coz you need space for what the future
Has in store for you

'Mi a con fuse' by Janette Bryan

Mi a con fuse, let mi tell yuh wah gwan.
Evry bady hav dem fyace pon book
Anna write don bout dem life an shear
Evry bady want tablit, is all a dem sick?
But dema talk bout dem cyan write pon it
A how many wod dem can put pon It
Mi nah ander styan disya worl
Evry bady a walk pon streeet
Loking pon dem hand,
Dem hav dis tiny ting
Dem a lok pon and a say dem a mek plan.
Oh laud den some tune start play
An dem put it to dem ear
Or even wors dem start talk to dis white tring
Hangin from dem ear
Dem a lauf and cuss an mek play dyate
To meet at one Mr Macdonalds
Dem seh dem gwan eat, byoy wat a cheek
If I knew him mi wod warn him dem comin
De yout of today mi na undastan
Wi dem book an tablit an man
And di ting in dem han dem a use a mek plan
Mi ah go hom and go sleep

'Severe Weather Warning' by Paul Delaware

Severe weather warning?
Please somebody tell me,
How do you define severe?
Meteorological equations?
Speed and degrees?
The wind last night was no light breeze.
Hostel full, service closed, shelter lost.
Alone, exposed, breathing frost.
Cut to the bone, soaked to the skin.
Shelter was found in a wheelie-Bin.
Relentless rain kept hammering down
On the metal, so sharp the rattling sound.
No sleep, curled tight, rigid and mean
Garbage bags that leaked oil and rancid cream
Gritted teeth, the bags embraced as a duvet
5 hours straight until the break of day.
Fear at every second.

'To this a happy ending?' by Paul Delaware

Brain, strain, walk in the rain,
Day, hard, stumbling, sick
Bickering, self, life, shit
Drunk, man, treacherous can
No love, no money, no plan.

Scream, anger, fight, street
Blood, vomit, call the police
Friends, family, never meet
Prison, bars, pleasure cease.

Soul, destroyed, courage gone
Pay, repent, forever wrong.
Rehab, relentless, cringe, fall
Relapse, shame, shrink, crawl.

Dark, lonely, struggle, sad
Diagnosis? Crazy, lazy or mad
Home, job and hope undone
Who will save this prodigal son?

Then, connection, trust, found
Soon, inspiration, solid ground
Peer support, future, make
Friends, laughing, coffee and cake.

'Self-healing' by Paul Delaware

Now, to face up and confront all my fears
And wallow no longer in futile tears
Philosophy has always been my close friend
Eloquent consolations for the brain to mend
"God is dead", "I think therefore I am"
To question is the definition of a free man.
I know that I know nothing
But a brief moment of understanding
Gives epiphanies and clarity of mind
Healing in words that shine
And love and empathy….. in time.

Craig Part Two

English Rose

My English Rose,
But does she know the beauty that is inside?
And can she find my naked eye
As it searches for her face so pretty.
The depth of warmth,
That she taunts from my soul of pity
Can rise and shine in my mind.
Her song I hear so fitting,
A living dream that I see across
A room of broken means, this vibe I hide.
I know she sees the man in me, it's like I'm amazing.
The sun chases the moon but all I do is stare,
The stars in line,
I wonder who really put them there.
I read these books but I can't turn the page.
I walk these streets but they're full of rage.
The colours merged my straight lines
Where curved my words.
I've learned the mention of her name
And I am unnerved.
How was I supposed to know the energy
That did flow would pull my mind apart?

Can I spend my right to be close?
I wonder if she knows the electricity
That flows from my toes to my nose.
She soon becomes my hero.
She is my mite blindness to sight,
My breath, my air, my immortal laid bare.
Every sense is alive, is aware
I am longing for her capture.
The skies will open with thunderous rapture.
My faith is her colour and with a chance
Doesn't mean that I cannot find the courage
To tie a knot and move in close to my English Rose.

Faces

Faces, people, souls, we are all travelling
Significant moments missed
Right in front of us as they are happening.
What are we conveying?
That long lost look, lost forever.
Don't be sad for we shared it together.
In that moment nothing was broken.
We walk our way through this life's maze
But we never forgot to give each other that gaze,
Even though we would never do it again.
I guess we were just restoring some faith in a stare
And there may come hardship little one
But this you will bear.
You will always see danger
So go ahead talk to a stranger,
After all most of us are not strange.
I don't know I can give you any advice
I know you got your own hand
And you will roll your own dice,
But if I could it would be this –
Stay open love, do not miss,
Create something every day

And please never ever forget to play,
Treat each day as a gift.
So never look down, your own face must lift.
Be yourself, your feelings do not hide,
But most importantly, enjoy the ride.
Hold a hand and help others to stand
And never forget to share a special stare.
You were in a pushchair. I was at a bus stop,
Just standing there and as your mother
Took you off that bus
There were 40 years in between of us.
Nothing was old,
Everything was new for I saw myself
It was me that was you.
I don't know if anyone else saw our stare!
I guess it was just letting you know
I will always be there.

Give Us

It is said that people need love
When they least deserve it, for that will impact.
Gratitude is not a feeling it is an act.
I ask you this, what do you attract?
From the dawn of age
We separate each other with selfish space
Or we try and chase a fantasy which is a lie.
So
Give us a status, give us a photo
Give us an existence, give us a who?
Give us the truth, take away the lie.
Give us humility or the ability to try.
Give us faith over hope any day.
Thank you for the strength to carry the pain.

Have you back

I need to part of the plan and grow in stature
Become a man I need to stand tall,
And not fall like the others
As they sold their soul for a gram.
So this one's for you my missing comrades
The ones I wish we could still hold hands for

I see you every now and then,
Either in an empty seat
Or on the corner of a busy street.
And I feel you in the wind;
See your face in the setting sun, on a beach
But my word you're not so out of reach.
I miss your annoying voice;
I wish you still had a choice,
I ask what this is all about,
I miss you shout
I miss the smell of your BO;
I miss the hair hanging from your nose
I miss your dirty nails. I miss every single detail.
I miss your silly tattoos.
I miss you telling me the truth.

The memories will live forever,
You touched my heart.
I even miss your fart.
I miss your outspoken opinion,
Sometimes rude
I miss your childish silly moods,
Not forgetting the way you chewed your food.
I miss your scattyness and your raggy clothes.
I miss everything, I miss your bones

See some might see all the things I miss,
Obscene and rude
But I'd have them back in a heartbeat,
I'd have you
So Danny D, Justin C, Rich B and Jeff D
I'll never forget what you mean to me
And for that it's you I'll always see
In the sky flying free.

How bad do you want it

When you can't go on
And it feels like your life is in tatters
Remember that you matter
When you can't see any light
And you feel your life is wasted
Remember you are the greatest
When you feel like throwing in the towel
And life seems to be too tough
You can do anything, you must look up.
I can't do it = bullshit, how much do you want it?
I will stand; life's battles don't always go
To the stronger or faster man
Sooner or later the man who wins
Is the man who thinks he can.
You may be alone right now,
But when you don't give up, you are truly found.
Will you live in a world that is made for you?
Or will you make your own world
That is brave and true?
You may open your eyes and feel hurt and pain,
But that's not the truth, you can win for the day.
If there is no enemy within

Then the enemy outside
Can do us no harm,
So when life knocks you down
Land on your back cos if you can look up,
You can get up.
Confucius said: 'He who said he can't
And he who said he can
Are, unusual, both right',
Make your dreams come alive'.
How bad do you want it!
Del Trotter also said
'He who dares wins.'

I got the lyrics

I got the lyrics
They run through my veins
But my mouth shuts up;
They got stuck in my brain
The voices and beliefs
Need reconnecting and rearranged
I look deep within
And relight my inner flame
But if God's son died in vain,
Then I'll see you again.
But do I really need to explain
The pen becomes my friend,
Some call it anarchy,
I call it apathy; I'm the judge,
Lawyer and referee
I'm just the only unluckiest bird in the sky
But I got a beautiful mind
So I try write the next line,
While you sniff a line
You won't cry, you try and hide,
You just fight ya pride
Need to take a flight to another time

Where there's no dark only light.

But love takes flight,
I'm alone at night
I grip the mic tight
And spit what I write
I strive to be alive
But I got the devils beast right behind
My spirits so alive
I could take on the globe
I swallow the fear
But it gets stuck in my throat
I'm putting my heart
Under the microscope
I'm looking so hard
But my blood's lost its hope.

It's all mathematics
I add and subtract
But I'm giving life
Backward I only see ends
In my neighbourhood
It's not a could, it's not a would, it's not a should
It's something that I've vowed
I'm gonna make my mum so proud

Invisible Voices now we're loud.

The pen dances across the paper and tells a story
PG18 is the category
Child welfare no inventory
With an education deformity
Yet his tutoring will surely,
Somehow, immortally
Be engraved on the unlawfully
And the dream catching disorderly
Who break free from the security
Of wanting arms that were never there
At this young age
He's probably showing
An us and them psychology,
So subconsciously
Sowing future years
Of burning apologies

With a desire to rewind
To the time where this character
Realised the emptiness
He was idealised under a street light
There was no one there and yet this shaming
Aimless road he would travel

Would split his soul
On the jagged sin shaped gravel
Distortion, grow in the battle with the barrel
Bones crying for release would rattle;
The spear would pierce through the fear,
And the mothers' grief would disappear,
The aftermath so severe
The pipe has no feeling,
The pin has no healing,
The smashing of the spirit brings kneeling,
Sun setting only weeping,
Truth from his lips are cheating
Time after time this creation is lost;
He ties his own rope,
With his mothers and fathers hands
Protecting his throat
But this affection is not owned
The gun is set for reload
Self-respect burns
Into the myth of yesterday's episode
But these, where his dark times were,
Nothing rhymed, he was possessed.
The burning unrest soon was confessed,
So his dreams could manifest.

How simple, he only wanted to accept the rest.
How perfect with the softest lens
In life he sets his own composure,
The torment is over
And now he carries a message of warmth by day
And watches his pen perform by night.

I know what's going to happen

How could she tell? She had all that power
She controlled my heart within an hour.
How was I supposed to know
The energy that flowed would pull my mind apart?
Can I spend my right to be close?
I wonder if she knows
The electricity that flows
From my toes to my nose.
She soon becomes my hero.
The wound that has passed her terrorist blast,
That tore through my heart, internal last.
Do not set my vigour adrift
She has slowed my pace down
She has straightened out my frown
Lost before her eyes I am now found
I'm alive with her grin; she sets fire to my adrenaline
Her innocence erodes across my skin,
There lays my end
And she knows my begin
This executes my darkness and restores my light,
Two morals unite
My ego takes flight,

She is now my mite blindness to sight,

My breath, my air,

My immortal soul laid bare

Every sense is alive, is aware my longing for her

I am in capture

The skies open with thunderous rapture

My faith is now her culture.

In my city

See, this is my theory; my mind is like this city
There's a park I go to when I want to be free
There are flowers there
And it's pretty with swings and slides
I can be a child and be silly
Across the other part of town
Is where I was lost then found
It was a dark night;
I tried to write but in went the knife
They stitched me up with the fear inside,
The city was warm for 5 minutes, my tears died.
I would stand on a hill of false pride

On the horizon I'd see a wall
And over, that dreams of the countryside
It was the pain of past years I was trying to hide.
I had to act the way I came across,
Looked like a magician
Being scared and lonely was my only vision,
Soul scorched, burnt in my prison.
In this city people seemed to be on a mission,
All over the place with no precision
I was searching for my rhythm.

In my city the roads were paved
With parking meters of hurt
It wasn't my money I'd insert.
For release I had to find my own church,
This is where I'd write,
The fear and freedom
Would merge the nursery rhymes
And lovers leaving seemed so blurred.
I didn't come first not even third.
See you don't wanna know my pity;
You sure as hell wanna leave my city.

In my city there is a beach,
The only place I get release
Where the pain and hurt I can delete
And the waves that crash
Are perfect and complete.
Then I go back to my sinister stare,
My face comes across like 'be aware'.
I see the words written on every building
And every lair
All I can think about is 'is this fair'
I can't escape the city anywhere

But is this really my theory?
Or is it the fear talking?
I ain't thinking clearly.

Woman You

It's like you wanna row with me
So my defences come up,
My hurt you cannot see
I can hear it in your voice,
It's like I never made you rejoice
And you kinda don't give me a choice.
I react in a way I don't like
And it's not a might that I've got my fist clenched,
That I might strike.
Cos my soul is split. I could never hit.
I love you, that's why I became a poet,
I'm not like those other men you know,
And you know it.

You saw something in me that was clear
And I see in your eye a tear,
But please look at me, I'm covered with fear
Maybe I didn't get that across so clear.
I'm totally fucked; I'm totally lost,
I don't wanna lose you at any cost.
I tried so hard to get close but I sense a frost.

See, I don't mean the things I say,
I wish I could've put it a different way.
I can't work out what's going on inside
I'm struggling to find out
The inner workings of my mind.
Vacant, I longed to be found out and redesigned.
It's like a judge has sentenced me
To eternal damnation with no time.
I've studied days, I've wasted hours,
I've brought her love, I've bought her flowers.

So I walk through my mind
And I try to find the reasons why she said goodbye
She said 'just go', how was I to know
That when I walked I'd never see her again,
Was that a game?
It was me she tamed.
I wonder if she ever says my name?
With each passing day my thoughts do stray
I long to find a way,
Where others will call us "they."
And as those words left my regretting tongue,
Powerless to stop, like the setting sun,
I saw the words pierce her like a desert eagle gun,

And if this argument continues I'll reload, and
Maybe I'll find the next line that really flows.
I took photos of her but she lied through the lens,
She pretended to be my friend and that wasn't her.
She told her status I was off key
So I walked away, not for her, but for me.
So let's put this warmth back
And let passion rule the track
In to me you see – that's intimacy.
It was always clever and true
The strength of a woman that was always you.

Second Friendly Interlude

**Poetry by R.M. Bodley, Jovannah Bär
& Nils Nisse Visser**

'The Fox' by R.M. Bodley

I called you
My fantasy woman,
My dream,
My fantasy,
My lie.

The deals offered.
Hope to be entwined.
Face my reality,
My place,
My story.

It can't be struck,
Can't make love stick,
Not anointed,
Unkind,
Disjointed.

The truth told,
On deaf ears fell.
Let go my fears,
My cares,
My tears.

Accept, I tried,
All those years.
Can't hide
Destroy
Belie.

The life led,
Needs unmet,
In action and deed,
I've blamed
I've raged,
I've shamed.

The fox, his message,
Honesty can't deny
My deceit,
My story,
My belief.

'Wailing wings' by R.M. Bodley

Under the wailing wings
Broken-hearted in their shade
I hunker.
My keening sings of all mine
And of others.
Brick by brick
So many, the list long
Fall away from the name wall.

The mortar no longer holds their place.
They take flight,
Their journey grace,
And a piece of me goes with them.
Forever lost, but not to my song.
By your paint,
By your pen,
Our hearts reminded.

Not too whim nor whimper,
Celebrate,
Eulogise.
How they touched our lives.
Only now are we true.

Think only of them,
Ourselves forgotten.
I miss them now we've no more time.

'What is Love?' by Jovannah Bär

What is Love?
There might be a hundred kinds of love,
And it's more than just an emotion.
I can't define it, though I've tried.
Love is so very painful when it's not replied.
Love can be a teacher,
Love can push you off-track.
Love is unconditional,
You cannot take true love back.

There might be a hundred kinds of love,
and it's more than just a state of being.
I can't explain it, though I've tried,
Love isn't over once a loved one has died.
Love can be a motive,
Love can be a shield.
Love is a two-edged weapon,
The scar remains a weak spot
Even after the wound has healed.

To me, love mostly travels one way,
I give them my heart

And then they run away.
While my love is loyal,
Love has made me strong.
Love's made me able to absorb hate,
Love's watched over me all along,
the loveless road I've travelled,
It's taught me to truly see,
If I want to be loved by someone,
Love has to start with me.

'Vae Victis' by Nils Nisse Visser

Once upon a time I yearned to fight,
Drag the despicable into the light
Filled with the spunk and spirit of youth
So utterly convinced I knew the truth
Passions, ideals, my future seemed wide open
Now I'm old, tired, beaten and broken
Youth's song of bright hope
Now fills me with jealousy
I belch and fart,
Scratch my arse,
Aged beyond,
Graceful remedy.

'Hopeless Romantic Shizzle' by Nils Nisse Visser

The light breeze causes the leaves to whisper
Of days, weeks, months, years
Forever ago and longer
When time did not rush by
In segmented ticks and tocks
But flowed in the free manner of a stream
Sometimes burbling by content and serene
Or else in a temporary dance of rush
Round and round over boulder and rock
And former majesty of fallen tree
Time wasn't measured by the merciless advance
And rhythm of mechanical seconds
But by heartbeat, dawn and noon,
Twilight and starry skies.
The slow passing of earth's seasons.
Circular and inexorable much alike that stern clock
But dawn's sunrise is far more kind and radiant
Than the insistent beeping
Up and down the street
Summoning all and sundry
from sweet dreams of freedom.

'Somewhen' by Nils Nisse Visser

Somewhen, summer's warmth lends me the urge
To forego adulting altogether, give in to the music,
Tap, turn, launch, leap, spin and land
In careless dance, around we go
Hand-in-hand with you in flowered summer dress,
Then wander aimlessly beneath the shade of trees,
To emerge refreshed in the hot sun's blaze,
For play, howl Sioux war cries, prowl like a tiger,
Without abandon, fierce and free in childish glee.

Craig Part Three

Judge

How many of you stare?
I mean how many of you really care
Putting the world to rights
Kicking back in your reclining chair
Channel 4 Undateables, is that really fair?
Benefit Street, Welfare, Healthcare,
Lottery be aware
Body shockers you're in need of repair
Deal or no Deal, Fantasy Millionaire
Your life expectancy is getting shorter
But no need to panic cos you got Skys Q recorder
You could be overcoming depersonalisation disorder
Don't waste ya time
Or turn your back on your daughter
Hold her, stronger and for longer
Be someone's supporter
A faith restorer, power importer
Head held high walker cross any border
Pray for your shoulder to be broader
Cos what can be the matter
When we judge a certain character
When we haven't see the previous chapters

Of pain suppressed soon turns to anger

And worried about their stature

So becomes madder

Not true to oneself, how sadder.

Look all around you and see the suffering

No one can hear your voice

You're fucking muttering

Your words about others are shuddering

You can't judge peoples pain, their recovering.

The world ends tomorrow,

Ya pride and ego swallowed

wonga.com, quickly borrow

Sing Ed Sheeran House of Lego

Social networking who you follow

Big Bang embryo ultra-scan

Audio sweet nothings from ya Romeo

But love, more than likely, gets KO'd

The streets becoming fatal

Gangster to Readers Digest Coco

Pharaoh dressed in gold

That's someone's hero

Air Max 9S in the ghetto

Ya not Robert de Niro

Could be Art Deco or totally retro

Fuck it

Read all about it in the morning Metro.

Little One

Her name runs through my brain,
Her love through my veins
But I go on, my body acts insane,
Will it ever be the same,
Can I live with fame?
I keep searching, when long ago I was merking.
The thoughts are loud,
I wonder if she is proud – of me
I reflect on what I attract,
How much of my life I act
My heart is broken - that's a fact.
Not in a way that it can't beat,
But in a way that I long to see,
That's my little girl, her name is Maicie
The fight is strong
Until I can call her and I, call us we.
She's in my prayers late at night,
Then I kiss the sky for her in the morning light.
Let me tell you she gives me energy,
With her at the forefront of my mind
I have no enemies.
I grow up in a street war academy

I stand with a mic, now you see me.

I can sit here with many woes,

Old life that is what I really chose.

I will never resist and moan,

Look at my fucking face it's totally toned.

Now I'll never be alone,

My left hand is glued to my phone.

I'll wait for her to call

Till then, I just wanted all of you to know

Maicie will always be a gift from this rounded world,

My spectacular, glorious, majestic little girl.

Meditate

My dreams are fleeting
I close my eyes
I fly away through the stars
To a place with no fear, no scars
I leave my mind with this earthly time
Children's laughter, the sweetest of sounds
Paradise revealed, angels and colours are all around.
I communicate in ways that are brave and true
I wipe loneliness from the sky, the script is new
The natural order to my journey –
The real hell is my life gone wrong
It's not about understanding;
It's about not giving up my thoughts
Don't race sky blue, is the sky I'm tasting
I'm the guy who is winning
I've closed my eyes at the sun more than once
Look into my soul, I'm giving a signal
My tears of joy are more than a ripple
A tsunami of peace is released
Tender my being for she has made me – me.

Mick 'E's Night Out

My friend Mick lives with a broken heart
Needle and fix,
He knows the streets and all the latest tricks
He builds a wall around him
With vodka bottles as bricks
He attends a karate class to protect his arse
No comment interviews, he's no grass
He steals antiques, he polishes brass,
His house is always dark
He's got a tattoo across his heart.
At weekends there is a one mil hanging out his arm
He carries a knife and commits pure harm
He smokes his weed in a bong.
His stories of breaking free from the ghetto are long
He's trying his best but he's highly strung
Didn't know his father and disowned by his mum
One day he was getting high with a homeless guy
He watched him OD
He watched him die
The police came by and asked him why
But Mick just lied like he did all his life
See Mick was accustomed to pain and loss

He grew up in the school of hard knocks
And struggled getting his feelings across
He would smoke them away
Through the pipe and the rocks
Mick decided to hit his mate for a sub.
He thought I deserve a night at a club,
Not before he sank a few at his local pub

He got in line and searched at the door,
Soon he was in
Some E he wanted to score,
On the hunt he looked out for a dealer
In the corner he found the boredom healer
He told Mick 'They're hard-core' and do him the job
So Mick opened his mouth and soon popped.
Within an hour it started at his feet,
Soon he was rushing and moving to every beat
The DJ set up a proper groove
Around the dance floor.
Mick swiftly moved,
He got a thirst and was drinking lots of beer
Few more pills down his neck,
Mick wasn't thinking very clear
He got some front, started chatting up this girl,

But he was chatting shit out his head, she could tell.
He told his mate 'I love you'
He was so out of his head
But then he thought
What the fuck have I just said.

Mick was feeling fine;
He got right into the DJs mix
Mick was on the dancefloor
Pulling off some wicked gymnastics
He looked at his watch;
All Mick saw was a haze
He tried to find the toilets
But felt like he was in a maze.
He spotted that girl who he bought an E
After a few hours kissing he realised,
She was really a he.

Miss James

I'm holding on to fragments of us
I just can't let go
I'm calling out your name;
I'm falling, cold and alone
Don't know if this is a dream
Or I'm wide awake,
I'm watching my life fall apart
I'm trying but I break,
The words written across my bedroom wall
Tell our story then fall
I try to piece them altogether
I tell you I'm sorry in a love letter,
But I never post it.
To make it better.
I must be out of mind
I count minutes
I count time
I'm longing for your love;
I really miss your touch
I wonder if you say my name much.

My life

See – My life is my life and your life is your life
But surely that's not how it's meant to be
Cos when I look at you, I'm really looking at me
An I know deep down within its beauty that I see,
For that to be real I gotta find the courage and tell
I see suns setting in your eyes and oh how we gel
This ain't a one night stand in a backstreet hotel.

And as sure as hell,
It ain't a lifer writing a poem in his prison cell
It's the way our eyes merge into two
It's you girl,
For you've pulled me out of this creation of hell
My spirit is adrift in your sky of liberty
When I'm in your arms I'm in riches never poverty
Gold, silver and myrrh
Fall from the skies like confetti
When you're away
I'm sent to a grave, emotional place
Where I long to come home to your welcoming face.
I'm inside you and my eternity is in total grace
There is no span, there is no space.

We come together

Like a rapturing crescendo of never ending song

You have put the right into my, oh so much wrong.

Let's not get this thing stale, lets push this along

So here I am trying to describe

This grandeur at its fineness

My joy, my light, my exhilaration

Are in total congress.

You radiate my skin, you are my dress,

My creator has sent you, my spirit spells bless

I am not young, I am not old,

In this time I am in perfect prime

The planets and stars are in unequalled line.

See my life is your life and your life is mine.

My Mindboxes

There are rooms in my mind,
Some of which I don't like,
I play with them
Move them from side to side
Some I try to hide
It's like each box has an infinity of locks
As a child I felt lost,
As an adult the fear hasn't stopped
In the box of regret there is a terrible threat,
It's getting bigger and it's swelling my head.
I tried to express my nervous disposition
In Born and Bred.
My family didn't talk to me
Nothing was said.
At night I would fantasize being switched off,
Like I was dead.
Being in prison wasn't the worst place
My tears were shed
It was being locked in my mind
With the terrifying boxes
I needed to bolt the locks,
They always infiltrated me from behind

I would try to explain it was when I talked,
That's when the boxes would squawk.
They screamed at me like finger nails
Down a chalk board
I visualise the violence that I saw,
The abandonment of a loner walking out the door.
If only I had said this – the regret would roar
Then one day I met her, my daughter
All of a sudden the panic became shorter.
It was like I could see as pure as water
I was glad I found her
But still the boxes rattled and got louder
It started again;
My fiancée disowned me as her friend
No more could I pretend,
These boxes needed smashing open
So this fear could end.
I couldn't believe it by far,
My waste of days,
My bloodline had gone away.

Beachy Head, over the edge
In between I'd lay
But something pulled me back

Was it one of the boxes?
Yes, written on the box was attract
And that's what my mind had always done.
Was it the behaviour set by my mum?
I would re-enact the things I witnessed when young
I needed to go back and make peace with this one.
I was on the verge of a new history for it had begun
It needed to begin soon for I knew
I was repeating a self-fulfilling prophecy of doom
Not only was my mind hurting from all the boxes,
My head had run out of room
And there it was I could finally see,
I had left my daughter as my father had left me.

My Time, Email

I don't wanna be a stat,
No more this society's doormat
I want to stand and be counted
Not by the amount
That's building up a bank account
Or Facebook followers that I count
While I'm asleep
I worry about my internet speed
Morning comes I check my Twitter feed.
I got a wireless lead,
A credit card that pays with full speed
When I travel pictures of food
And people wanting a bath is what I read,
I put on a shirt just to go to work,
Having a cyber relationship I toy, I flirt
My Google search
Would equate to an internet pervert
I don't want to physically talk to someone,
I might get hurt
I mean I'm a Bluetooth,
Wi-Fi, usb, flash stick,
Modern day cyber expert

Check me out, I never have to post an email,
I follow the crowd
Wonga.com, money on bail,
Where debt seems to be fashionable.
I've evolved into a cretin of retail
I look outside myself,
My soul seems lost like it's for sale,
But my dreams are real.
I play the Lottery, giga bytes, inches on my HD telly,
Internet connection that's my priority.
I've no time to feel guilty,
There's food on the table for my family,
What more do they want from me.
I mean I see more of a pixel screen
Than a human face,
But let's put this into place.
I wake up early and join
A self -centred consuming race,
Where time is sold
And where a stranger will speak to me
Is a total disgrace.
I've the right to my own technical space.
I live in a time where I'm conditioned
To have myself on my mind, but the truth is!

What I really find is the most important commodity
That I own is time.
I need to put this wireless world to one side
And spend my time with my own kind
One day my hearts clock will take its final chime
And if I have not given true love
Then that would be
A lifetime of real crime.

This is me

I feel poisoned by these city lights
I've been a in a position to take flight
I miss the day, as my mind recalls
I've scars on my knees, I've stumbled, I fall
I've picked myself up more than once
I've been called stupid; I've been called a dunce
I've hurt many, I've hurt a few,
I've lived with Karma, now I'm new
I've shed a tear
I've lived through fear
I'm learning lots, I've had my lesson
I've told the truth in confession
I've lived with many, I've lived alone
I've travelled afar, I've longed for a home
I've listened to the sweetest of song
I've not stopped when I knew I was wrong
I've fallen in, I've fallen out
I've learned to whisper, I regretted my shout
I've taken a day; I've sat with a dream
I've controlled a scream, I've lived a scheme
I've longed to be alone, I've longed for a touch
I've lived with my hate.

I've never regretted love
I've given a life
I've asked two for a wife
I've risen from a place that's dark and down
I will never stop till my heart is full,
Till my heart is proud.

Third Friendly Interlude

**Poetry by Anthony Munk, Steffi O'Driscoll,
Robert Greig-Smith & Lesley Stoner**

'Undersouled' by Anthony Munk

I'll drink my way through the river of death,
Do all I can to disable my breath
I'll stone me down, down into the ground
I'll smack me up before I'm found
I don't want dragging out into the light
I'll stay in the hell of my dark sweet night
My well-worn armour tickles with rust
The warm corruption of shivers and dust
I can't be fussed with your empty hope
I'd rather make lust to my spirits and mope
But there's not much left of my soul to sell
There's no way out of my heavenly hell
A mild flirtation with Beachy Head
Might do the trick so the devil said...
I come to, swaying along
In a dreamy rum-drunk daze...

The seashore speaking from the foot of the cliffs
Beckons, repulses, rock-hard fluid,
Rhythmically gentle
Rustling tones to carry me off, lying,
Their promises of no return

Sounding empty as a broken bell.
No, they will return, they always have,
They always will, washing over and forever burying
The newly cooling corpse over and over and over.
I won't be there to hear their echo as in a shell.

Or will I? And will I, will I return?
Must I? Am I condemned to?
Dust to dust, sand to sand,
Maybe...
But will I be driven all the more violently back
Against the chalked-up walls
I'm doing all I can to overcome
In my selfish leap of unbelief?
Shelfish, yesh, sho it izh.
Shellfish will shellfishly gather,
Filter-feeding their way
Through the fragments
Of the aimlessness of an unexamined life.
Can anyone bring me, force me back to life?
Non-life is impotent to fulfil my death-wish,
A wish that is really a yearning for life,
For truth, for a way of love
That is stronger than death..

"Love does not depend on time",
On my inability to behave well
Or overcome my weaknesses.
Love is the power that stops at nothing
To accept us as we are, not as we aren't....
How real is that real truth
That is the desire of every human heart...?
It's nothing less than THE defenceless,
Immensest news:
I don't always have to have the blues
I may have walked for miles in my broken shoes
But now I know I have the need to choose
To draw the nearer to my hidden muse...

I'll ditch the stuff
That knocked the stuffing out of me
I'll choose the beauty that you've always given me
The beauty that I never thought I'd see
So plain it hurts but when it hurts I know I'm free
Freely free
Free to be
All of me
I may one day not be afraid to say I do
And if I do say yes to life because it's true

It will be all because what's mine is down to you..
So if you ever hear a holy voice knock at your door
You'll know you're loved
Because your heart longs to be pure..
A voice the like of which you've never heard before
It calls and calls and calls until you can no more
Be deaf or wilfully ignore
The voice within that knows that love alone is sure

'Warm stripe and gack train' by Steffi O'Driscoll

The air is thick with hope
That something will fill the void tonight
They find each other in the corners of the dance
Eyes wide
Cling tight
Scared of breaking the day alone
An unspoken bond is formed
A partner in crime to help forget
A hostage for a new dawn
The rave is over but this lot are not ready for bed
They are on the warm stripe and gack train
And there's a long journey ahead.

Same train Same destination
Same old tired conversations

"You're a cunt"
"No, you're a cunt"
"See you, I fucking love you"
The stragglers pile into the living room

This living room is my temporary home from home.

I laugh and tell them
"It's cool" not wanting to be the boring one.
170 bpm bottles of cheap white wine
And lines are on the go
"Do you want some love"
"Nah I'm alright as it goes"
Bass face already formed,
My armour for the day.
A sunrise of grotesque features
As I burn this morning's coffee and pray.

14 months ago I'd be with them
Trying to get off the train but missing all the stops
Waking up at the end of the line
Miles for the ends
Only to end up at the other end of the line
Again and again
But it's different today I'm not boarding

There's nothing for me here.
I'm bored of this. This is boring. I shower.
"No you fucking can't come in and have a piss"
I pray for strength that I can't get out of this.
I don't want to be around it,

I finally accept it and own it.

You don't have to pretend

If they're your real friends they'll understand it.

You have a choice now

Pack your suitcase get the fuck out of here

There's a place not too far away

Where the coffee is good and the stories are rich

Where you can put pen to paper and exorcise this.

'Drunken Roads' by Robert Greig-Smith

Beg at street corners cross roads raise their
Rifle trail whites crossed words tune in
And out in wires and dark and shared
Tea read in leaves, junctions, bones. In

Lanes where mice pace spaces shadow draws out
Paranoia voyeurs, freighted time voids
The hum out cast, out lawed; drums out shouts
Stilted in space, folding's in time, splitting

Second see conditions. E. I. C
Tree e,f,g tar and mac metonyms
Oil'n dear streets brick a black lane,
Lost street angels two corner mark angles.

Intel see hear I pad I steer each trace
Between to tread where right left scaffold dead,
Street corners, cross worlds, puzzled words face
Cities bright white lines left to right.

'PEACE' by Lesley Stoner

What good will it do? They seek no wisdom.
Did not the master teach them long ago?
And in the years that pass, with bind indifference
They care not to know,
But in the thunder of disintegration
Let the red life flow.
A deep affliction of maladjustment
In the human mind
Beneath the canopy of intellect
Asserts itself through all the long experience,
Always to reflect this deadly malady -
Each generation seething to affect.
From the far start before the words were formed,
Aggression smouldered in the hearts of men,
They, to that mindless Lord with strange obedience
Swore allegiance then;
Then - as today, the curse of every nation
Festered like a wen.
Sorry are they - in their chronic sickness.
Should the omnipotent crush and renew?
There is no hope in this for worlds willed ignorance
While there are so few
Ever to profit from stark revelation,
What good will it do?

'Shades of the daffodils' by Lesley Stoner

Ten thousand storms I saw in just a glance
Capped by the brown distemper of decay.
One solitary bloom remained to dance
In sad remembrance of yesterday.
In words unbidden, solace I conveyed:
For natures transiency I voiced regret.
And as I spoke the blossom gently swayed,
Concurring with a nod, I see it yet.
Now, when I think of that lone, wilting life
That stayed so short a spell in sun and rain,
I cannot help reflecting how the strife
Of man from age to age is all in vain.
From that unhappy scene there came to me
"The still, sad music of humanity".

Craig Part Four

Separated

I share my dinner with a dog
But oh how we like to snog

I share my bed with a rat
Where is he when I want to chat?

I share my nights with a spider
We do like to laugh when drinking cider

I share my garden with a mole
My god has he really got a soul

I share my bath with a trout
And trust me he does like to shout

I share my car with a donkey
And he can't drive straight, it's all wonky

I share my time with a horse
And when he bolts I get coarse

I share my sofa with a bear

I caught him once in my underwear

I share my conversations with a snake
But sometimes I sense lies, he seems fake

I share my love with a fish
Sometimes I think this is foolish

I share my life with a mouse
When we split up, who will keep the house?

Shopping for a life

Welcome to your life.
Long shopping list.
Choose wisely for on your death bed
You won't want to regret or miss
And the more you hoard
The more you will diminish.
Let's have it right,
It's a list you may not even finish –
So let's go straight to the shop.
Oh dear, not a good start,
Your list you've dropped or forgot
You'll have to ad lib.
Now don't forget to check, peoples,
Best before on every lid now
There's a packet of regret,
A tin of pain and a loaf of self-pity.
Some mushrooms looking distressed,
Bananas feeling depressed,
An oddly shape carrot looking disorientated
There's a charge for your weight,
Oh look a lonesome looking date,
But it's not on your list,

How does that equate?

You ain't got time for that or was it fate?

On this shopping journey

You may seek some assistance,

Don't feel shy, no need for resistance

Just remember your self-worth

These issues of life,

Have plenty of girth,

You can cover any distance.

You may even need a hand to reach the top shelf,

That's the adult section

You may need to read that one by yourself.

With self-indulgence you will need plenty of it

Insecure corn on the cob.

I can't remember how the next line goes, I forgot.

On this shopping trip

your basket or trolley may collide or hit,

Someone from your past that's been torn or split.

Your dignity will show in how you deal with it.

There be no need to feel timid

Whether you're filling up your trolley, basket or bag

Maybe trying to grab a life with both hands

Don't try and steal your meal cos it's all tagged

In the last checkout lines it will all be scanned

So who brought all the goods to the store?
They all arrived in a lorry,
For the goods have fed and clothed our naked body.
Keep your receipt; it's your memory, your only copy
So your belongings in your bag you do pack,
A journey of shopping
As you look back, you see a sign 'Please come back,
You could win a holiday if you give us feedback'
But deep down you know you're not coming back.
The things you've packed you can't take with you
When the light turns to black.
As you wait your turn,
Love and tolerance you will learn,
Even though the old woman in front
Makes your patience burn,
Show respect. She's completed her life's
Adventurous shopping journey
She'll never return,
Now your shopping journey will end for good,
Will you be happy with your goods.
Will you stand at the final checkout
With your trolley full of could, would or should?
Did you keep your own fire burning
With satisfied kindling or grateful cheery wood?

So ask yourself if your shopping trip is truly real,
For the items you feel, come with such a good deal
Or is it expense to be healed,
Either way will there be anyone at your table
For your final meal?
The average life long shopping list in years is 84.9,
That seems a long time.
M.I.N.E. that spells mine.
What are you really giving not taking,
Do you see the sign, or do you sit staring at a screen
Fuck that shopping list – I'll do mine online.

Street Man

Street man stuck with his can,
He can't stand
The war races
Disgust on their faces
As they pass him by
He drinks, he stinks
No one fucking thinks
He's someone's only son
'It's not my battle
As they float by him like cattle
In the midnight hour no one sees his rattle
The soul that sits adrift
In the abyss with a clenched fist
Is screaming for some love
And this could be ya mother, ya sister,
father or brother
But no, you think of another
And it's more than likely you
Street man without his can
Watch him stand as you pass him your hand.

Take me away

Take me away from this council estate
Take me away from all this hate
Where I can create my own fate and love is made
Not where my burned out body is laid.
Take me away from this concrete can
Where the merchant has my life in his hand,
So I can withstand the seduction of the golden sand
And not drown in a reservoir of faded dreams afar
And my unborn shines brighter than any star
Take me away from this synthetic block
Where a father will sell his soul for a rock,
And this baby is born with a lock to its liberation
But the key is lost.
Take me away from this immoral province
Where this child will look to its drunkard prophets
With empty pockets and mis-sold promises.
Take me away from this soulless penitentiary
Where benefit street seems to be temporary
But in truth it's been going on for centuries.
Take me away from this ruthless jungle
Where off licences, pubs and bookies don't struggle
And the lost are scared to the bone of the knuckle
And empty tears are forming barren puddles,

Pull this rock down into rubble,
Self-worth, respect and dignity is given
But in truth it is took.
Take me away from this so called hood,
Where babyhood, childhood, adulthood,
Brotherhood, fatherhood and motherhood
Are totally misunderstood.
Take me away from this soulless city
Where so many hearts are filled only with pity
And lots of lessons are learned
In Her Majesty's University,
Young arms waiting for intimacy and security.
Take me away from this ungrateful ghetto
Where a child's cry for help is but an echo
And the depth for apathy is shallow.
Can't pay we'll take it away casts a shadow.
Take me away from this one man village
Where each morning one eye opens
To a terrifying image:
The poor being crushed by the rich
And love becomes a contraband
With a terrible shortage.
See, I've got a room with a little black box
That sits in the corner.

I don't know what it does to my brain
But my attention spans getting shorter,
Is it about the latest tricks?
I think I've become a conformer
But in the bosom of the darkest night
I become a performer.
This technical age psychosis
Keeps me in hypnosis
With no prognosis.
I'll make my own diagnosis.
Condition Denialtosis,
But I'll tell you this I was looking for a missus
So I signed up for plenty of fish.
I sent a cyber kiss to this blonde
But I think she saw my profile picture
And didn't want me then.
I got a message off a brunette.
Her name was Bernadette,
We were getting on well
And we haven't even met.
She told me she was on meds
To grow her chest and lose her biceps.
It's a good job I never met her.
It turned out her real name was Peter.

Time Wasters

This one goes out to all the time wasters,
The life passing them by
Long star gazers, stuck on the sofa complainers
With multimedia modern day behaviours
The ones that say do not enter my domain
With the head phones on
No talking on the train,
The ones that refrain
From saying their name
But quick to blame the ones
Talking or singing, thinking they're insane.

This one goes out to the ones that moan,
The ones that reap but forget to sow.
Always prone for a groan
With all their opinions and nothings they know,
Constantly gossiping on their phone.

This one goes out to the ones with the false belief,
The ones that never change the side of the leaf.
The fresh air thieves,
The fascist comments on others they unleash.

This one goes out to the reality TV watchers
With the mind paralysing remote postures,
The vaper smokers, popcorn lung coughers;
Buy anything to make them feel better shoppers,
Benefit street scoffers,
Job centre scholars.

See, some people are like boats
While some are sailing others just float;
Many preach, others quote,
Out at sea with wind in their sail
Or stuck in a harbour boat like in a jail.
Deep blue sea or run aground,
Some are swimming and others drown.

See, some boats are shiny and sturdy
Whilst under the water they're scared and dirty.
I like boats. I'd like to have one of my own
One that glides through the water.
I can travel oceans, I'll be an explorer.
I will discover long lost lands
I'll leave my footprints in the sand
And build my own boat with my hands.
I'll even design my own flag.
Not all boats are the same,

Some will be given a name,
Some will be given fame.
All will let in water but only a few will drain.
Boats are a bit like people.
Some are bought on PayPal
And some are given a label
Some go alone
While some are proud and naval,
But most importantly it's in how we sail.

Two will merge

And this was when she touched me,
My soul was set free
And I could finally be the man
I was truly meant to be.
Electricity was flowing through my mind
Her juicy wet lips tasted like
Life's sweetest nectar wine
Prison bars were smashed
I'd actually found my time.
The words she spoke were finer than Mozart,
Pure rhythm, pure rhyme.
This girl was all mine.
She kissed and caressed my neck,
Then moved down to my chest
Like Adam and Eve we were naked, undressed
With no hesitation I touched her breast
This wasn't a test, and I definitely wasn't her guest.
She had my attention under total arrest.
I was out at sea and her body (and her)
I was about conquest
My mind (my mind) is racing;
I need to keep it real

Two will merge into one,

That was the deal.

I stand at her golden altar then I kneel.

She knows my secrets;

She's undone my masculine seal

Like a firework exploding pure vibrant colour,

That's how I feel.

Our bodies shook, our eyes locked, the world spun.

We lay there still;

I could not describe this vibe, this thrill

Refined ecstasy, her mind was intoxicating,

Stronger than any man made pill.

This wasn't a game.

She will never put me down like a disused toy.

We were two elements, the strongest of alloy.

I was her joy, for she had turned me

Into a man from a boy.

Unbreakable Are We

Lonely am I here
Away from her, not near
Questions asked why
I do not see again then die
Come back what I know
True dreams will show
Scented sweet flower
So I long each hour
What bridges my broken heart?
Unbeaten maps I do chart
I search for her since birth
For her grace sweeps this earth
Lonely am I here
For her I shed a tear
One day joined and connected
Where nothing will reject it.

Undone

Mastermind as I try to find a key to a puzzle.
I just can't deny it's not the trut
That will set me free
It's knowing my makers mind and his belief
It's burning me, the unrest is clear
It's something in my voice; it's me that I fear.
My eyes tell a story, sweet are my tears
My soul casts no shadow; I'm lost to the years.
I'm given some power and I sense some light
I push on with all my might.
No questions are asked.
I don't need to fight worldwide news
That terrifies my searching pupil,
That justifies a homeless soul,
Street corner that occupies
Lost in the snake pit
Trading an eye for an eye.
I wake each day and take my turn
A clock on a wall alone,
It burns on the edge of a cliff, no point of return
So I force open this closed door for her
I worship and adore.

Forgiveness came in the shape of a sycamore
I'll never return to the pain from before
I will not condemn the less fortunate ones
Divide and rule, separating the sun
The shell of my pride and my ego will come undone.

Where it's made

And here is where it's made.
Street corners and dark alleyways.
Money for paranoia is the trade.
Shooters, dealers, barons getting paid
An this is massive, it's in ya neighbourhood.
Its next door, it's where ya live
An you can be passive or even aggressive.
Either way it ain't cheap. It's expensive.
In ya minds eye, don't forget to blink
Yahoo hacking information,
Sync the streets are weeping,
We must remember words are failing,
Rumours are spread, the lost are found,
To the walking dead trust is given.
Make it great again it said.
Eyes wide shut
Alone we are led, media making us judge,
At least not you -
Comments unleashed
Without walking in their shoes,
Front page news.
But is it all true and in this world of twisted faces

The streets are racing,
The paper chasing from hand to hand.
Even McDonalds black suit security
Manned energy drinks for the kids,
Sugar equating to cocaine in a can,
Advertising making self-destruction
Look so appealing.
Telling us we're broken and in need of healing,
Natural looks need rebuilding.
Ego, pride only brings kneeling
Broken families in need of feeding
Death wish warrants soon bring stealing
Paying that bill
Swallowing a pill
Learning to chill
But ya can't keep still
Police soon grill
Fuck ya will
Chase that thrill
Or even that girl.

Wordsmith

As a wordsmith am I meant to bring you a message?
Like a story in my life's passage
But I don't know the words
And I don't know the language
I was born at a disadvantage
So get your mind's eye to this image
I dream of being taken away by an alien race
Where they surround me at my feet, they praise
And a multitude of bright colours shine,
Beam from my face.

As a lyricist am I meant to work from a script?
Souls talk to me from the other side and their crypt.
From billions of people on this planet,
But it was me they picked
And as the bright lights blinded my eyes
I was taken to a place beyond this life
Where I could see the decline
And death of mankind.

What were these future beings making me see?
And yet it seemed clear to me

People were losing their dignity
Stepping over each other
For the invention of money
I saw my own chase on a nightly
Maybe this journey was for me
To make peace with myself -
Pretty unlikely!

The air was still, not even a breeze
These beings were pure with no disease
For the first time in my life I had time to reflect
I saw it all from a different aspect
Like the Knox effect.
Irregular particles are varied
While my column diameter was fixed
I was warm, I was alight,
My mind's eye fell though this vortex
What I was about to see was this

They started to show me the early stages
Of our history
It all seemed a mystery
But I could soon see man's self-fulfilling misery.
I saw Jesus feed the 12

And if they didn't want to
Follow him they were going to hell
I soon realised these humans
Had no faith in themselves
I had a total separation from this planet's desires
I saw the Romans
And different countries build these empires
They went to war, I can't believe what I saw.

Man's love for each other in total divorce
Millions would die, millions would mourn
Then came the technical age
And this just suppressed man's rage
They talked to screens and not each other's face
I was taking in so much it was hurting my mind
I had no concept of space or time
They told me the only way of getting somewhere
Was leaving something behind
But this image was screened through my mind's eye
And the message I was receiving was,
I was born to be redesigned.

Streets

I look at passing strangers
Faces wishing I were they
And they were me
But I put on a brave face
As if I'm in disguise
Regret and shame is what I visualise
I live on Benefit Street
I wish I could hide
Trapped in a system that shuts my mind
Surely this is the final cut
I mean my life
How will I edit
Has the universe really given me credit?
An advantage that something brings
That is a true benefit
But I ain't feeling it
How can I make a start?
How can I make a start?

Acknowledgements

The Oaks
Dawn, Jason, Joe,Liam, Ricky, Lee

You pulled me through when I couldn't pull myself.
Thank you.

I owe a great deal of thanks to the following:
God, my mother June Neesam, Ron Neesam my father, Vicky, Matthew, Elaine, Garry, Jane, Shelby, Natasha, Sarah, Laura, Cathryn, Leanne J, Poppy, Maicie, Wayne G, Marc S, Coleen, Summer, Donna, Daisy Lynn, Emma, Stuart, Ashley, Kate, Sarah M, Mandy, Zoe H, Charlie, Paul F, Wayne H, Love Removals, Neil, Andy S, Chris, my buddy Gary, Brian, Dan W, Sarah I, Leanne F, J Swan, Nils, Jovannah, Cascade Recovery Café, Invisible Voices, Parkhill Church, BHT, No. 5, Steff O'Driscoll and Kate Tempest

Proof reading by Janet and John Going.

Special Thanks and RIP

Glynis
Sadie
Elvis Monaghan
Jeff D
Justin C
Danny D
Naved
Margaret
Ian (What a touch)